Metaphors & Similes You Can Eat

And 12 More Poetry Writing Lessons

by Orel Protopopescu

SCHOLASTIC
PROFESSIONAL BOOKS

NEW YORK • TORONTO • LONDON • AUCKLAND • SYDNEY
MEXICO CITY • NEW DELHI • HONG KONG • BUENOS AIRES

DEDICATION

Dedicated to the teachers who welcomed me into their classrooms and the students who revealed to me the potential of my own ideas.

To Siyu Liu, artist and friend, who introduced me to the art of "shi" poetry.

ACKNOWLEDGMENTS

"Willow Song" was reprinted from *A THOUSAND PEAKS, POEMS FROM CHINA* by Siyu Liu and Orel Protopopescu, published by Pacific View Press, Berkeley, CA, 2002.

"Living Tenderly" by May Swenson. From *THE COMPLETE POEMS TO SOLVE* by May Swenson. Used with permission of the Literary Estate of May Swenson.

"Waterfall" by Samuel Menashe. From *THE NICHE NARROWS: NEW AND SELECTED POEMS* by Samuel Menashe. Copyright © 2000 by Samuel Menashe. Reprinted by permission of Samuel Menashe.

"Instant Storm" by X.J. Kennedy from *TO THE MOON AND BACK: A COLLECTION OF POEMS* compiled by Nancy Larrick. New York: Delacorte Press, 1991.

Every attempt was made to locate the authors of the model poems. Please feel free to contact the author with any further information.

Orel Protopopescu is always happy to hear from students and teachers. You can write to her at: P.O. Box 709, Miller Place, NY 11764.

Cover design by Norma Ortiz
Interior design by Solutions by Design, Inc.

ISBN: 0-439-44511-6

Table of Contents

Introduction

I began teaching children to write poetry when my older daughter, Xenia, was in second grade. Because her fine motor skills had not developed as quickly as her verbal abilities, she did not like the physical process of writing. Today, even small children learn to type on the computer, but then (1985) families were just beginning to acquire personal computers. I decided to start a writing club for my daughter and two of her friends, so that they would write with as much pleasure as they read. I didn't realize then that I was starting a whole new career. A collection of poems by the Turkish poet, Nazim Hikmet, is entitled *Things I Didn't Know I Loved*. Teaching young children to write was one of those things for me. I had taught composition to college freshmen as a graduate student and high school English as a student teacher, but never imagined the joy I would find in nurturing the poems, plays, and stories of younger writers.

We met on Saturday mornings for an hour at first, and soon expanded to two hours. Others heard about our club and asked to join. Their parents didn't pay for the lessons and I didn't give grades, yet the children wrote and wrote. The club lasted for years, even after I was already doing workshops in the schools as a visiting author. Some of the poetry lessons in this book were first tried out in our writing club. Kenneth Koch's books on teaching the young to write poetry suggested an approach that I still use. I never give students a specific topic, just a concept (such as giving voice to something that can't speak for itself) and I often get these ideas (as Koch did) from literary models.

Sometimes I create the models. I've been reading my "Knows" poems (about what something not human knows) to students for years. A student's poem, "Blue Knows," inspired me to write a book of color poems. So the circle of inspiration rolls, from teacher to student and back again.

I have learned from all my students, whether they were deemed "average," or "gifted" or placed in "special education" classes. In the world of poetry, these distinctions are meaningless. Poetry is its own special education.

Public school students, some from "special education" classes, wrote nearly all the poems in this book. Teachers of every grade and ability level have shared with me their astonishment at what even their most reluctant writers have produced in my workshops.

Lessons to Unlock Creativity

A fourth grader, after I had visited her classroom several times, told me, "Now I see poems everywhere." My hope is that you and your students, after exploring just a few lessons in this book, will see poems everywhere, too.

How does it happen? To paraphrase the early twentieth-century Russian educational psychologist Lev Vygotsky, I don't teach in the zone of my students' actual development but to where I know they can go. These lessons provide what Vygotsky called the scaffolding that helps students reach heights of expression they might not be able to achieve without it. Each lesson with its basic steps is a tool for unlocking individual creativity. Although I use

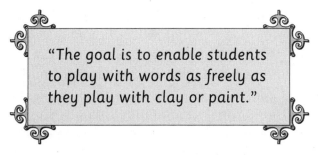
models, my goal is not to have the students mimic the model, but to fully absorb it, so they can soar.

I know these lessons will work in your classroom, because they are designed to eliminate self-consciousness and literal thinking, two enemies of poetry. Think of them as word games with loose rules. Present the lesson, the rules of the game, but let your students know they are free to break them so long as they stick to the general idea. These lessons are springboards from which students can do somersaults or belly flops, as they wish. Some may walk to the end of the diving board, peer at their own reflections, and, paralyzed by self-consciousness, do nothing. Don't worry if your students have trouble writing on a given day. It happens to all of us. One cannot always measure the success of a lesson by what's on the page. It's impossible to measure the subtle shift of a soul. The goal is to enable students to play with words as freely as they play with clay or paint.

At the end of every lesson, reserve at least ten minutes for volunteers to read their poems aloud. I never force anyone to read and always have more volunteers than I can accommodate. Struggling young writers, inspired by the work of their classmates, will often catch fire at the last minute and finish their work at home.

The Role of Editing and Revision

Most of the poems in this book were written exactly as presented here, needing little editing. Many fourth to eighth graders, however, benefit from more extensive oral and/or written feedback. They often don't have the experience to recognize their most original ideas and develop them. After all, when you're young, almost everything is new. When I see an exciting idea, I'm eager to share my enthusiasm with the student, helping him or her to bring the rest of the poem up to that level. I sense the poem that's waiting to be born, and become its midwife, helping it into the world.

Students often express gratitude when I show them how to enhance their work with editing. By helping them to see a poem in a new way, I'm training them to edit without me. As Vygotsky pointed out, appropriately modeled behavior becomes self-regulated. The goal isn't to get them to revise a poem the way I would but to build on what I was able to show them. The greatest reward is seeing your students discover your own

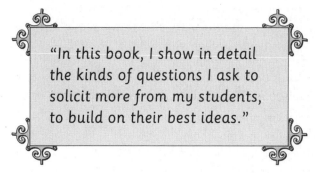
fallibility. I helped my daughters edit their work when they were small (and still do, when asked), but now they're young women who give me excellent feedback on my own writing.

Children are natural poets because they

love to play. The same love of play makes them natural editors, too. The best suggestions a teacher can make are those that help them play a little longer. Always try to elicit a little more. "What kind?" is a question that grows adjectives, whatever the noun. I've seen "an embryo moon" and a "fingernail moon" thanks to my asking "What kind of moon?" If you want more verbs, more movement in the poem, ask "What's it doing?" In this book, I show in detail the kinds of questions I ask to elicit more from my students, to build on their best ideas. I also show my suggested cuts, which students, of course, are always free to ignore, and often do! I don't feel that I am changing their work by editing it, but helping it to breathe. After all, adult writers rely on editors. When you help your students edit their work, make it clear that they own it, regardless of your opinion. They always have the last word.

I know that this point of view is controversial. There is a trend in schools today to rely on peer review, eliminating a teacher's input. At its worst, this process can result in pooled ignorance, but when properly monitored, students can be trained to focus on the positive. Peer critiquing is best done with a teacher present, to counteract any negativity. Students are often naturally keen editors with a good sense of what's missing from a poem or story. This ability does improve with practice. But all students can benefit from the intelligent input of an adult who appreciates poetry. I always learn from teachers whose classrooms I visit, and have met many who enjoy writing along with their students. Happily, several teachers allowed me to include their poems in this book.

If you are uneasy about revising, apart from spelling and grammar corrections, this book will help you gain confidence.

Reading the first and final drafts of the student model poems will help you master the process. Sharing the "before" and "after" versions with your students would be a good way to introduce the topic of revision. You will undoubtedly notice things I missed. That is as it should be since the revision process is no more absolute than the process of writing. It can be just as joyful. Nothing pleases me more than to see a student respond to one of my questions with a wonderful new idea.

Whenever I help young people revise their poems, it is with deep appreciation and respect. I can only hope, someday, to write as freely as my students, whose work never fails to touch and inspire me. As Picasso said, "It takes a long time to become young."

Writing More Than Poetry

Poetry can prime the pump for all kinds of writing, both fiction and nonfiction. Using similar techniques, I've had students write "voice" stories as well as poems. When I teach metaphor, I often read prose fiction as well as poetry, so students don't think of metaphor as only a "poetic" ornament. It is the heart, soul, and stomach of literature, so I recommend starting with my appetizer lesson, *Metaphors and Similes You Can Eat*.

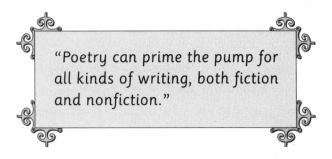

"Poetry can prime the pump for all kinds of writing, both fiction and nonfiction."

Metaphors & Similes You Can Eat

Since the poetic ability to make comparisons (metaphors and similes) comes from the imagination stimulated by the senses, this is a good lesson with which to start a poetry unit. You can use any finger food, but I prefer to use fruit, a different type with each class, for variety. Kiwis are particularly evocative. Bananas are the easiest to peel and cut.

You will need:

- ❀ Fruit (at least six pieces per class)
- ❀ Paper plates (for cutting and displaying fruit)
- ❀ Sharp knives (handled only by teacher and/or assistant)
- ❀ Napkins or paper towels
- ❀ A copy of the reproducible for each student (page 9)

Start by having students work in groups of six or less. Give each group a fruit to study, placing it on a plate in the center of a round table or grouped desks. Hand each child a copy of the reproducible on page 9. Have students fill in the title (name of fruit) and their own names. Go through the five senses in order, starting with how the fruit looks and feels on the outside. Ask them to pretend they've never seen or tasted this fruit before. Have them hold the fruit with their eyes closed. If they didn't know it was a fruit, what would they think it was just by touch? What does it

sound like when you peel/slice it? What does it look like on the inside? Ask questions to elicit more detailed descriptions. For instance, if a child says or writes that a kiwi looks like a potato, I'll ask, "What kind of potato?" Then the child will usually add an adjective, such as "a hairy potato."

TEACHER TIP

Make sure students respond with nouns (metaphors and similes) and not adjectives. If you get a response like "feels slimy," for example, ask them, "Slimy as a ......?" Encourage students to write down more than one response for each section. I have been astonished by the original similes I've gotten from young students. I asked a class to complete the phrase "round as...." A five-year-old girl said, "love." I asked, "In what ways is love round?" She answered, "Like this," making a circle with her arms, fingers interlaced, "like a hug."

When they've completed all five senses, have them think of a question that no one else in the world would think to ask the fruit. They can address the fruit by any name or title they wish. A second grader (my younger daughter, Nuria) wrote: "Mr. Orange, are you really orange, or is that only a mask?" Another class came up with, "If we leave you alone for a long time, Miss Banana, will you be sad and go bad?" Have students write more than one question, if possible.

Finally, invite students to look over their responses and choose their best images to turn into finished poems. The model poems on page 10, as well as the suggestions on "How to Rewrite Your Poems" (page 64), should help. (Read only those poems not about the fruit you're using, to avoid inadvertent copying.) The model poems were written by students who used the worksheet first and then selected their best images for the poems. They were minimally edited by removing articles or repetitions. When the poems are done, students enjoy reading them aloud. It's fun to see the variety of ideas generated by the same subject.

Sometimes, before the class writes, I'll bring in red delicious apples and pass them around, asking the class what they might think they were if they didn't know they were apples. What do they look like, feel like? I go through nearly all the steps on the worksheet on page 9 (skipping smell and taste) but rapidly, without writing the responses down. After slicing the apples in half so they can see inside, I'll jump straight to the questions they might ask the apple or about the apple.

Then I'll share my poem:

*A*pple

You're like a red vase
holding one brown stem,
like a short, fat candle
that swallowed its flame,
like clouds of stars
on a deep red sun,
setting behind
my green bowl's rim.
You're smooth as wax,
as glass, as bone,
but inside you're slick
as a mossy stone.
Two white moths
live in your heart.
Their spots are your seeds,
shiny and dark.
How many must grow,
how many must die,
before one tiny seed
sprouts a tree, so high,
it plants hard red apples
in a soft blue sky?

—Orel Protopopescu

Students listen attentively to see if any of their observations mirror my own, as they often do. I may read the poem again, pointing out the "clouds of stars" (white dots on the surface of the apple) or the white moths I saw inside each sliced half. Then I give them a different fruit to write about. You may want to try edible flowers, like roses or squash blossoms, instead of fruit.

Name _____ Date _____

Metaphors and Similes

_____
Title

On the outside, you look like _____

_____

_____

You feel like _____

_____

When I peel you, you sound like _____

_____

When I slice you, you sound like _____

_____

Inside you look like _____

_____

_____

You feel like _____

_____

You smell like _____

_____

You taste like _____

_____

Tell me, _____, _____

_____ ?

Model Poems

Banana

You look like the bottom of a boat
And feel like a new bar of soap.
When I rub you, you sound
Like someone carving wood.
You feel slimy inside
And taste sweet and sour,
But smell like a distant perfume.
Why do you have the same color as the moon?

—Elizabeth (3rd)

REVISION NOTE: In her first version, Elizabeth had simply written "perfume." I asked her, "What kind of perfume?" She added the adjective "distant," which goes so well with her question.

Kiwi

A kiwi is a small planet,
spinning through space,
staring into oblivion,
waiting in silence
to shed its sour surface,
to show its inner sweetness.

It sheds, silently,
like a mouse tiptoeing
on an ever quiet sky.

Inside, a story is told
of a star where many planets
get pulled to a fiery doom,
like a magnet pulling iron filings
to a center ever so sweet.

—David (5th)

DISCUSSION: Similes are comparisons using the words *like* or *as*. Metaphors are like similes, but don't use those words. The first line of Elizabeth's poem contains a simile; David's first line is a metaphor. He expands it in the lines that follow. Can you find other similes or metaphors in these poems? How would you turn a simile into a metaphor or a metaphor into a simile?

Ways of Sensing

With students in grades four and up, I extend the idea of looking at something with all the senses to topics other than fruit. I might still bring in apples and do a mini-lesson first (see page 7), but I will let them choose any topic they wish to look at in multiple ways, as in Wallace Stevens's famous poem, "Thirteen Ways of Looking at a Blackbird." The following examples were inspired by student models (see pages 13 and 14), not Wallace Stevens's poem.

TEACHER TIP

For an excellent analysis of Stevens's poem and its use in the middle grade classroom, see Kenneth Koch's book *Rose, Where Did You Get That Red?* Koch analyzes the variety of approaches Stevens brings to the subject: a narrative, a question, a stage play, a math problem, etc.

 Make copies of the words on pages 29 and 30 for the word box (see page 20).

 Explain to students that they are going to write poems in which they describe one subject in as many ways as they can.

 I begin by taking a word from the word box. I lead students through a short group poem first, writing the "ways" on the board, then asking the class to help me select the best ones. Here are two sample group poems.

Peony

White, fluffy cloud
drooping over sun,
white, silky blanket
covering sleepy children,
whipped cream,
cotton ball,
Milky Way swirling
up in space…
Why does your head
hang low?
Lift your perfumed head
and look at the sun,
your mother.

—Mrs. Schaer's class (6th),
Longwood Middle School

Door

A gateway to a new world,
It swings like wind.
A wooden giant blocking my path,
Why do you cry when I close you?

—Mrs. Looney's class (5th)
Chippewa Elementary

Then share this student-written poem.

To Look At a Morning Glory

1

A blue piece of sky
that sleeps in the night
and wakes up with the sun.

2

A genuine piece of silk
planted in a garden.

3

What do you dream of
when you sleep with the sun?

—Brittany Latronica (4th)

To enrich this process, ask questions. For example, in the poem "Peony" on page 11, I heard "cloud" and asked, "What kind?" which yielded some adjectives. (This same question applied to "head" obtained "perfumed.") "What's the cloud doing?" elicited the word "drooping." I asked, "Drooping where?" (I might have asked "how"?) By constant questioning, I show the class how to develop ideas. When I suggested they command the flower to do something, someone told it to lift its head and look at the sun. "What is the sun to the flower?" A student suggested "mother," the last word in our poem.

Even though I call this lesson "Ways of Sensing," I find that if I don't bring in fruit or flowers, if the students can't touch or smell the subject of the poem, they tend to rely on visual images. Write all five senses on the board and encourage students to use them, but don't oblige them to use all five. Some may delight in imagining the taste of the stars, while the more literal-minded will refuse to open their

metaphorical mouths. Don't worry. Ask the holdouts to write about why they refuse to taste stars or flowers or even kiwis. The world needs all kinds of poets, even those who refuse "poetry." If you meet resistance, join it! Suggest an opening line, such as "Star, I won't taste you, because…"

With younger students, you may prefer to use the model poems on pages 13 and 14, from fourth through sixth graders. These were only lightly edited. In most cases, we selected the best of the "ways" from slightly longer poems. Comments on other aspects of the writing process follow each poem, where relevant. Ask your students to write as many "ways" as they wish, bearing in mind that quality is more important than quantity.

Here's another poem to share with students.

Four Ways to Look at the Grass

1

Grass is a great blanket,
soft and perfect, just for you.

2

A home for bugs and worms.

3

Grass is the thin child
of Mother Nature.

4

Grass is a seed
that can make
the world green.

—Daniel Naja (4th)

When Daniel was composing this poem, I asked him to add at least one describing word, or even a whole line, to show us what "this child" looks like. That's when he added the word "thin."

Model Poems

Seven Ways of Looking at the Moon

1

The window in the night
Lets us glimpse the brightness
Of the coming day.

How is the moon like a window? Where is its light coming from?

2

The round shiny seal
Holds the ends
Of the black envelope together.

What is the "black envelope" that the moon is holding together? What kind of "seal" is the moon being compared to?

3

When the orange flame
Is extinguished in the black water,
All that is left
Is a white round candle.

What "orange flame" is extinguished at the end of each day? What does the "white round candle" refer to?

4

When you are lost in the blackness,
The moon sends down a soft arm
To comfort you and point out the way.

What is the "soft arm" of the moon?

5

The light at the end of the pendulum
Arcs back and forth across the night,
Hypnotizing the world to sleep.

How is the moon like a light at the end of a pendulum?

6

The day shrinks
Until all that is left
Is a bright spot
Surrounded by nothingness.

In what ways is the moon what's left of a shrinking day?

7

The eye of the night
Surveys its sleeping children.

—Xenia Protopopescu (9th)

If the moon is the night's eye, what is the night's heart, breath, voice? (Poetic questions with an infinite number of answers.)

Three Ways of Looking at an Egg

1

A little white chest
without a key,
holding gold
for you and me.

2

White and gray
and polka dot.
Some have more than
just one spot.

3

White as a cloud,
smooth as a stone,
round as a ball,
treasure bound.

—Vincent Russo (4th)

Three Ways to Look at a Cloud

1

A white pillow
for a giant
to sleep on.

2

White cotton candy
in the sky
for a carnival
nearby.

3

A white piece
of loose-leaf
crumpled up,
leaving blue stripes
in the sky.

—Robby Russo (5th)

Five Ways of Seeing Stars

1

Little lightning bugs
trapped in the sky.

2

A dark field growing
small pieces of gold
which die when the sun
spills its light.

3

Stars, why do you
never dance
with the sun?

4

Your firing lights
guide us
through dark nights
when the moon
is sleeping.

5

You're stuck in a prison,
little pieces of the sun
that join together in the day.

—Christa Nussbaum (5th)

Hide the Metaphor

This lesson is designed to help students expand a metaphor. It's important to stress that metaphor is the soul of literature, both poetry and prose. To make this point, I often read Mark Twain's description of his character, Colonel Grangerford, taken from the first paragraph of Chapter 18 of *The Adventures of Huckleberry Finn*, in which the man's personality is described in terms of weather:

> "...Everybody loved to have him around, too; he was sunshine most always—I mean he made it seem like good weather. When he turned into a cloud bank it was awful dark for half a minute, and that was enough; there wouldn't nothing go wrong again for a week."

Explain to your students that a metaphor is not a definition like "A tiger is a big cat," nor a fact like "Snow is water in a different form." They should also avoid confusing images, such as "The sun is a big grapefruit, ripening in the sunshine."

Ask them to play "hide the metaphor" with this example from an anonymous student: "The night is a stream/with stripes across the sky./ When it thunders/ the water is hitting the rocks./ As the comets go by/ is the stream flowing." How would you make the comparison clear without stating it explicitly? Ask the students to describe night as if it were a stream. You might start them off with a few lines: "The night flows, rushing over rocks and stars…"

Then ask them to try to write a hidden metaphor, to describe something as if it were something else. You might suggest (especially to those who seem stuck) that they think of an animal without naming it, as in the poem "Fog" by Carl Sandburg. Have the students read the poem aloud and try to guess which animals are being compared. Students might also do the reverse, describing an animal as if it were a person (lion as king of the jungle, for example) or a natural phenomenon.

Fog

The fog comes
on little cat feet.

it sits looking
over harbor and city
on silent haunches
and then moves on.

—Carl Sandburg

Ask your students, "Is fog described as if it were a cat in this poem, or is a cat described as if it were fog?" The answer may seem obvious, but it's important to make it clear that the poet was describing fog while thinking cat. That's the trickiest part for young students to absorb. Sandburg never names the cat, though he gives a strong hint with "little cat feet."

The nouns compared in a metaphor should be close enough that the comparison makes sense, but far enough apart that it's interesting to bring them together. Ask your students whether fog/cat meets this test. They are certainly far enough apart, but what are the similarities? Write three of the five senses on the board (see, hear, and touch) and ask the class for similarities: Fog and a cat look fluffy and can have similar colors, too. They are silent. While you can't hold the fog, it gives you a soft feeling, and it moves like a cat, stealthily. Movement is a sensation akin to touch.

Personification is one of the easiest forms of metaphor to grasp. All students will enjoy Hagar Shirman's poem (page 18) in which a ball gown and man's evening costume meet in a dry cleaning shop. Even the youngest students will understand that the clothes personify a woman and a man. They might be inspired to invent their own characters. Also, see the poem "Darkness" on page 34, in which darkness is described as a hungry creature, devouring light.

Some students find it difficult to expand a metaphor. Give them the option of writing a series of metaphors that describe one subject, such as "Love is…." Try a group poem with the class, to warm up. You may want to read these two short poems I wrote, all rhyming metaphors, and ask which is an expanded metaphor (January) and which a series of metaphors (March) on one subject, so the distinction is clear. Ask them to find the three metaphors in the "March" poem.

These selections are from *A Lake's a Cake, A Calendar of Poems*:

January

A lake's a cake
You slice
With your skates when it is ice
Too thick to splinter,
Where you figure-eight
To decorate
Winter.

March

A kite's a sprite
You guide,
A bright message
That you've tied
And sent by cable,
A designer sky's
Lift-all-eyes
Label.

You may need to explain to students born in the digital age that messages used to be sent by cable, that is, over telegraph wires.

Model Poems

The Rain Breakdance

I drop like the rain
and throw my legs
like rain slipping
off the roof.
I step after step
like the drip drop of rain.
I do a twist
like rain in the wind
and end the dance
on my knee in a puddle.

—Timothy Nowicke (4th)

The Queen of Summer

Summer is a queen
Ruling the whole world,
Bringing beauty to the Earth.
Its crown is full of flowers
And all that comes at summer.
The birds sing just for her,
Sing a summer song.
Her skin is smooth and warm
And her heart shines brightly.

—Fiorella Torro (4th)

DISCUSSION: "The Queen of Summer" expands one metaphor. "Spring" contains a series of metaphors on one subject. Do you think the comparison of spring with a mummy works? Why or why not?

Winter's Wings

Winter flies in,
Its giant wings flapping,
Blowing cool winds with a
    whoosh.
It flutters around,
Blocking the sun,
Leaving white feathers behind.

—John Giblin (4th)

DISCUSSION: Can you find the metaphors and similes in these poems? Which ones are hidden?

Spring

Spring is a mummy being unwrapped
    from its white linen,
The shedding of winter,
When all life regains its color.
Spring is a scarlet macaw,
    joyfully colored,
An uncontrollable life, sprouting
    from the ground.

—Jeremiah Regan (6th)

Velcro Love

They were put together
The way a child puts on Velcro
    shoes.
They could be separated
As if a child ripped them off.
They kissed like Velcro strips
    touching,
But after a while, they got worn out.

—Joey Trabona (5th)

Inside a Dry Cleaning Shop

Inside a dry cleaning shop,
They met each other on the rack.
Him so manly and so neat,
From the top of his hat
To the cuffs of his slacks,
So dark and handsome,
Tall and sleek.
Her so dainty and so pale,
With plump arms topped with lace,
A waist so tiny, tied so tight,
With a ribbon of the purest white
From which flowed a skirt,
So wide on every side,
His sleeves started to shake,
His heart flip-flopped,
His jacket stretched,
And two buttons popped.
He tipped his hat and asked,
"Where did you come from?"
"From the Governor's Ball," she answered.
"And you?"
"A wedding," he replied.

Inside a secondhand store,
They met each other on the shelf.
Him—ragged and a little torn,
His hat all crumpled up,
Four buttons missing and a sleeve,
And his bow tie gone.
Her—without the lace and all the bows,
Her white ribbon, a dirty yellow,
Her arms just hanging like a sack,
Her worn skirt drooping at the back.
"We meet again," he sadly said.
"Yes," she sobbed,
But more she couldn't say,
For then the trashman came
And dragged her far away.

                     —Hagar Shirman (7th)

 # Panther Night

The night is a panther
blacker than black.
It prowls the earth
as the sun goes down.
It quiets the world
with its pitch black dark
as everyone sleeps
and dreams good dreams.
The dark is silent
and swift and large
and up in space
it surrounds the stars.

            —Andrew Stein (5th)

REVISION NOTE: Andrew's last two lines originally read "It's up in space and surrounds the stars." I suggested switching "and" and "it('s)" to continue the flow of thought from the previous line.

 # Moon

The moon is like a peach,
sometimes whole,
sometimes half,
sweet like the night sky,
growing each day.

                —Kristyn Wynnyckyi (6th)

DISCUSSION: Hagar crumpled up this prize-winning poem and threw it away. I rescued it and helped her shape the final draft. The dress and formal suit of clothes (she and he) are metaphors for what? Can you find the one simile in this poem?

Startling Combinations

This lesson demands the same kind of abstract thinking that expanding a metaphor does. Students will pair two nouns or a noun and adjective to create a kind of friction between the words. Use it to supplement and reinforce the previous lesson or as an alternative for students who are having trouble grasping the concept of a metaphor. Metaphors often emerge from this exercise naturally.

Start by reading to your students the following humorous poem, "Instant Storm," from *To The Moon and Back, A Collection of Poems*, compiled by Nancy Larrick.

Instant Storm

One day in Thrift-Rite Supermart
My jaw dropped with wonder.
For there, right next to frozen peas,
Sat frozen French-fried thunder,
Vanilla-flavored lightning bolts,
Fresh-frozen raindrop rattle—
So I bought the stuff and hauled it home
And grabbed my copper kettle.

I'd cook me a mess of homemade storm!
But when it started melting,
The thunder shook my kitchen sink,
The ice-cold rain kept pelting,
Eight lightning bolts bounced round
    the room
And snapped my pancake turners—
What a blooming shame!
    Then a rainbow came
And spanned my two front burners.

—X. J. Kennedy

Although Kennedy's poem is light, the student poems inspired by it are not necessarily:

Silent War

In our hearts, a silent killer
In our eyes, a silent thriller
Wars kill us inside silently
After the silence is over
We break down
Loudly

—Sean Murphy (6th)

Copy the list of nouns and adjectives on the next page on the chalkboard or on chart paper. Students can add words to the list, then mix and match as they wish. Tell them they can pair nouns with adjectives or choose two nouns, but not two adjectives! Put them in two separate word boxes (see page 20), one for nouns and one for adjectives. If you like, add nouns from other lists in this book, or more words of your own.

NOUNS	ADJECTIVES
Dream	Broken
Love	Silent
Darkness	Falling
Rose	Peaceful
Storm	Sour
Words	Loud
Eyes	Instant
Winter	Rising
Spring	Cruel
Summer	Sweet
Fall	Wild
Lie	Silly
War	Mad
School	Scared
King	Tired
Day	Young
Boy	Old
Girl	Brilliant
Wings	Restless

If they use the noun/adjective pair, your students should choose words that create some friction between the adjective/ noun, not habitual language: *not* instant potatoes but instant storm…. *not* silent night but silent war…*not* young boy but old boy or old girl… *not* broken heart but broken dream…

Share "Silent Hurricane" with students and then share some of the model poems on page 21 with students.

Silent Hurricane

During the night,
the wind blew softly.
My dog didn't bark
as she usually did
when it was dark.
The wind was blowing
through my dog's hair.
I got up in the morning
to see if she was there.
In the yard,
there wasn't a sound,
not even the dog
moving around.
Now I know there was
a silent hurricane
in my heart
that night she died.

—Alicia LaMattina (6th)

MAKING A WORD BOX

This is a very useful tool for helping reluctant writers get started. When I first tried it, I naively thought it an original idea, but have since discovered that many creative teachers and writers have been using it for years. What always works for me has clearly worked for them, too. I've included suggested word lists for several of the lessons in this book (pages 29, 47, and 58). On these lists, I mixed abstract (love, hate) and concrete (paper, tree) nouns. This mixture is particularly useful for teaching metaphor.

Any small box or other receptacle will do. I use a colorful one that once held a pile of notepapers. Copy and cut apart the word lists for the lesson you're doing. Invite students to take a word from the word box. I like to make multiple copies of the word lists so there are duplicates of the words. This assures that two students will write on the same topic. Variations on a theme can be very instructive when the students share their poems. You may want to add your own nouns to mine, perhaps to reinforce a vocabulary lesson.

I store the words from each lesson in separate envelopes. When I am teaching a particular lesson, I take out the envelope of words I need and fill the box, taking care not to mix words from different lessons.

Model Poems

NOUN/NOUN PAIRS:

 ## Darkness Rose

Red rose, red rose.
Dark, red rose.
At night, a rose will bloom.
At day, a darkness rose—
Has bloomed.

—Adam T. (5th)

 ## Snow Clouds

In the sky and on the ground,
White lies everywhere.
In the sky are white clouds.
On the ground, white snow
looks as if clouds have fallen.

—Adam T. (5th)

 ## Paper in Water

As I sneak into the water pool,
A piece of paper falls in.
When the wind blows,
The paper moves like a boat.
Out at sea, the boat sinks
And falls deeper and deeper.
I catch it on my arm
And it's a cast.
As it dries, it writes
A letter with water.

—Christine Slatest (5th)

DISCUSSION: "Paper in Water" is not strictly speaking a noun/noun combination, as it's not about paper water or water paper, but that's beside the point. This student played with the notion of paper and water and came up with these poetic, memorable lines. As I said before, my rules are meant to be broken, especially when they break so beautifully.

 ## Midnight's Wheel

Midnight's wheel rolls
Around Saturn's rings,
Poor helpless people
Getting no sleep.
Blue and white here no longer
For the sky is black.
City slickers wander,
Yelling with the streets.
The planets are falling,
Making us weak,
Screeching moons
Becoming litter
In this black night's bloom
As the wheel rolls on.

—Adam Kahn (7th)

Voice Poems

Objects, feelings, and ideas talk in Voice poems. They are made to seem human. I start this lesson by asking students if they know what a ventriloquist does. After a brief discussion, explain that they will have a chance to be ventriloquists. Instead of using a dummy and making it speak, they will be giving a voice (in a poem) to anything in the universe except a person, since people can already talk for themselves.

Explain to students that we experience the world through our senses. List the five senses on the board, with corresponding body parts.

See . . . . . . eyes

Hear . . . . . ears

<u>**Feel**</u> . . . . . skin, nerves, hands, fingers, etc. heart, head, brain, mind, soul

Smell . . . . nose

Taste . . . . . tongue, mouth

I use *feel* instead of *touch* to stress the duality of feeling, both tactile and emotional. I usually underline the word *feel* since it's the one sense I don't want anyone to leave out of the poem.

Tell students that they can use these sensory words in order to give their object or feeling a voice. Of course, these are suggestions. No one should feel he or she has to include all of them in one poem.

Next, ask students for topics for a voice poem, letting them know that it doesn't have to be something one can see or touch. It could be a feeling (love, hate), an idea (success, failure), or any season, for example. You may want to use the words on pages 29 and 30 and the word box to help students find potential topics. Encourage students to pick something that they have strong feelings about, positive or negative, but don't discourage them from choosing a playful topic just for fun. (I do make one exception: cartoon characters. Since these are already personifications, they are excluded.)

Tell students that in these poems we are trying to make something not human seem human (personification). Therefore, the object, feeling, or idea can have anything a person has. As you explore possible topics, refer to the list of senses you wrote. Create a list of other body parts. *Book* naturally leads to the words *back* and *spine*. Whatever topic they choose, ask them to imagine it has all these parts. *What color is winter's hair? What's the heart of the sun like? Describe the moon's face.* These questions inevitably produce poetic answers. You can add *hair, face, blood, bones*, and so on to the list of words on the board. Remind students that their objects might also have other human attributes such as a family (mother, brother, father, sister), friends, enemies, likes and dislikes, fears and dreams.

 You can also suggest that they use similes and/or metaphors by adding:

My voice is/ is like...

My breath is/ is like...

My touch is/ is like...

My step is/ is like...

I move like...

Here you can substitute any qualities you like, taking suggestions from the class. Make it clear that the students don't have to use any or all of these, just the ones that stir their imaginations. Invite them to complete page 28 to brainstorm for ideas.

TEACHER TIP

Tell students, as I once heard the author Grace Paley say, to write what they don't know about what they know. In this case, it means their poems shouldn't tell us what we all know about shoes or stars, love or hate, but what these characters would tell us if they could speak.

Finally, share the following student-written voice poem. It has inspired students from first grade through junior high. After they've discussed the poem, encourage them to write their own.

Baseball

Shrieking across
The baseball field,
I fear
That cracking bat.
I don't have a say
About where I go or stay;
I would
If I had a mouth.
My heart is covered
With string and thread.
I don't know
If I'm alive or dead.
When I'm thrown,
I feel alone.

—David Normoyle (3rd)

Ask students why the poem would be less interesting if the boy had written, "I am a baseball/ you play with me/ the pitcher throws me and the batter hits me/ and I fly through the air/ into a mitt..." Even the youngest students can see that this is boring because it tells us what we already know, in language that is tired, not fresh.

I suggested that this student break lines for rhythm and rhyme, which he did. An alternative would be breaking lines for meaning at the end, to emphasize the meaning of the last word:

I feel
Alone.

Other model poems are found on pages 24 and 25.

Model Poems

 ## Whisper

You can hear me in school.
My foes are the notes you pass,
because they stop your whispering.
My friends are the ear and the mouth.
My dream is to travel,
whisper after whisper, afar.

—Kathleen McMahon (4th)

REVISION NOTE: The ending of Kathleen's first draft was: "My heart will break/if you stop whispering." I felt she needed to say something new at the end, not just echo what she'd written in the third line.

"It's hard to picture a whisper's heart breaking," I wrote on her paper. "What would destroy you? What would you wish for?" I always ask several questions, hoping one will inspire the student. In this case, the "wish" question inspired a wonderful "dream" ending. A dream or a wish often works well at the end of a poem.

 ## The Eraser's Song

You eat cookies, ice cream cones,
Dogs eat dog food, juicy bones,
Frogs eat flies, cats eat birds,
I lose weight by eating words!

Spell them wrong, my heart skips beats,
Your mistakes become my treats.
The more you write, the more I feed,
Eating words that you don't need.

Sliding, gliding on your page,
I begin to show my age,
Gray with words although I'm young,
Yummy on my gummy tongue.

Crunchy consonants are great.
Tempting vowels fill my plate.
Every word's a tasty gem.
I'd give up my life for them!

—Orel Protopopescu

DISCUSSION: What words in "The Eraser's Song" make the eraser seem human? (Hint: Think of your five senses.)

Mirror

I reflect the truth
that you have tried
to conceal.
I am immune to
your lies.
I am your equal.
A strike at me
will only cause you
damage.
Your image was
ruined when you
shattered me.

—Pete Speer (8th)

Leaf

Sitting on a tree all day long,
I lost track of who was around me.
We all look the same.
I always heard the wind shouting
as he passed by.
He sometimes frightened me.
I saw people running
as they played all day.
When they left,
open fields were all I could see.
I fell down one day
and there was no time to say good-bye.
I hated being alone
and cried all the time.
My friends, the crickets and the bees,
come and comfort me.
I dream of being back home.

—Allison McCann (4th)

Wind

I can scream like a banshee
In a storm,
Or whisper secrets no one
Can tell.
I can touch your neck
With icy fingers
And swirl around you
Like a mist.
I am terribly lonely,
But my rage at solitude
Is drowned out
In a tempest.
The only companions
I have are the songs
And the words and the screams
That I carry along.
I can drive harsh sand
Into your eyes
Or cool a humid summer day
With a breath of my breeze.

—Deborah Wassel (5th)

REVISION NOTE: In this poem I merely suggested tiny deletions, removing "filler" words that didn't contribute to sound and/or sense. A poem is a song. Instead of musical notes, its music is in words, their sounds and rhythms. Read your poem (aloud is best) and remove unnecessary words.

"I Am" Poems: A Variation on Voice

"I Am" poems are similar to "Voice" poems. Their structure is taken from the poem "Fire" by an anonymous 11-year-old girl, which was published in the book *Miracles, Poems by Children of the English-Speaking World.*

 Begin by reading the poem "Fire."

*F*ire

I am fire. You know me
For my warmth and light,
For my crackling, leaping
Colored light
Which comforts all.
I am fire. You know me
For my endless moving,
Burning, destroying hunger
Which eats all.
I am fire. I have one foe
Who conquers my might,
Who quenches my thirst,
Who swallows my light.

—Anonymous

Help students to see that those six words ("I am...../ You know me for....") set up a rhythm.

Then provide students with a copy of the reproducible on page 28. (You may want to make an overhead transparency of the page.) I find the structure is comforting to students and helps them get started. As they grow comfortable with the structure, students may then cut out the words "I am" and "you know me" if they feel they don't need them. Often, "I am" poems end up as voice poems. Sprinkle words from the word box (see page 20) on the desks of those who want them. Instead of ending with an enemy, many prefer to use a dream, as did the first grader, writing in the voice of the sun, who said, "...I have a dream/to stay up all night/and see my best friend, Moon."

If students use *friend* or *enemy*, prompt them to give a reason for the friendship or enmity. A second grader, writing in the voice of the rain, was prompted to say sun and rain were friends because "we make rainbows and help flowers grow."

Model Poems

Winter

I am winter.
You know me
for the white blanket
I lay upon you,
for the cold hard stare
I lock on you,
for the harsh breath
I blow on you.
I have one enemy.
She dances in her dress
of colorful flowers
across your lawn
after the sun melts
my blanket of snow.

—Dawn Eisenbraun (4th)

(This poem won first prize for poetry in the Eastern Suffolk County Reading Council Contest.)

Paper

I am paper.
I feel the words you put on me.
I see the pencil after you are done.
It looks like a needle
Coming to poke me.
It feels good to be written on,
To be used.
I fear being shredded.
I dream I'm folded
And I soar.

—Kenneth Harris (5th)

Candle

I am a candle
My wick sings through the center of my soul
The glow I emit melts my existence
Slowly
Painlessly
I am eternal for an unknown tomb
I am forbidden in the eyes of the blind
I am light at birth
I am smoke at death
I am a candle

—Erica Lussos (teacher, 4th)

Bees

We are bees.
You know us for
our stinging rays
which pierce your skin,
for our busy buzzing bodies
and our sticky hairy legs
which carry food.
We are bees.
You know us for our sweet-smelling honey
which busies bears.
We share one hive,
We share one dream:
To be the queen.

—Xenia Protopopescu (2nd)
Angela Lu (3rd)
Adrienne Lu (4th)

DISCUSSION: Poets often make up words. Did you know that the playwright and poet Shakespeare added thousands of words to the English language? When you use a word or words that suggest the sound of whatever the words are talking about, that is called onomatopoeia. Onomatopoeia is used throughout "Bees."

Voice or "I Am" Poems

I am _____

You know me for _____

My mother is _____

My father is _____

I was born in _____

I live _____

My best friend is _____

Because_____ (We like to) _____

My enemy is _____

Because _____

I fear_____

Because _____

I love _____

Because _____

I dream (or wish)_____

shadow	red	Mercury	car	July
echo	green	Saturn	mushroom	March
light	blue	space	anger	summer
dark	ice	snail	puppy	winter
lightning	snow	fish	jungle	spring
thunder	hunger	letter	forest	fall
joy	grape	paper	kitten	fly
sorrow	rose	baseball	cloud	bee
peach	daisy	football	scarecrow	mosquito
apple	tree	soccer ball	gold	bird
pear	pine	tennis racket	silver	seagull
plum	leaf	lily	cow	eagle
caterpillar	Mars	river	pig	lava
butterfly	Jupiter	ocean	horse	volcano
octopus	moon	stream	duck	tornado
salmon	sun	wave	chicken	hurricane
gorilla	star	jeep	January	pencil
yellow	earth	bus	September	paper

basketball	television	surfboard	cup	toad
bone	lobster	Velcro	canary	frog
lamb	tooth	fossil	parakeet	mirror
raccoon	rain	love	octopus	Venus
war	spider	hate	deer	glass
peace	airplane	rock	porpoise	truck
life	boat	bread	tiger	seal
death	deer	shell	monkey	computer
ant	brush	dust	earthworm	sea
book	comb	guitar	movie	shell
hammer	rabbit	violin	hand	rope
saw	hill	piano	thumb	happiness
drill	banana	chocolate	foot	green
poetry	ring	ice	nose	dream
art	storm	cream	chair	feather
dance	wolf	knife	table	lily pad
music	skate	fork	lie	coffee
radio	skateboard	spoon	wasp	tea

Note: Color words like *green* are used as nouns.

"Knows" Poems

I dropped my older daughter off at college and spent the night in a nearby motel. Waking up alone in that unfamiliar room, the words "a rose knows" swam into my consciousness. A silly idea, I thought, but then I remembered that several poems I admired began with seemingly silly ideas. I thought of Wallace Stevens's inauspicious opening, "I placed a jar in Tennessee," and Emily Dickinson's, "Hope is the thing with feathers..." Without hope of being as inventive as either of those poets, I decided to see, nevertheless, where those three little words might take me and my student poets.

Begin by reading this poem.

A Rose Knows

      how to grow
straight towards the light,
sipping the juice of earth
through a stem packed tight.

It knows how to show delight
and to show pain,
then tuck itself in, at night,
dreaming of sun and rain.

A rose knows how to glow
when it's admired,
and how, when inspiration goes,
to show it's tired.

It knows when to bloom
and when to blush
and when its day is done,
how to let go of its petals,
     one
        by
          one.

Explain to students that they do not have to imitate the rhyming in the poem, just the idea of relating, in a poem, what something that isn't human knows. The subject doesn't have to be concrete, like a rose. It could be an emotion, a color, or a concept like success or peace. Show them how the rose poem uses line breaks for rhythm, rhyme, and (in the last line) to underline the meaning of the words "one by one."

Share with the class your favorite "knows" poems from my students on pages 33 and 34. Then write these words on the board:

(A) _____ know(s) how to, when to, where to:

    grow, live, survive
    eat, drink
    work, play
    hide, seek
    give, take
    let (you)
    make (you)

show (you)
move, run, creep, fly, etc.
open, close
start, stop
remember, forget
love, hate
sleep, dream

As you can see, this lesson is built on verbs. These are some that have worked well for me, but it is just a starter list. I always ask students to add to the list as I'm writing, so I generally end up with at least a dozen more verbs, particularly in the movement category. Ask them about other ways of moving than those listed here.

Make it clear that they do not need to use all the verbs on the board in their poems, just those that suit their subjects. In the same way, they may want to use "how to" but not necessarily "when to" or "where to" before whatever verbs they choose. Once they get into the rhythm of the poem, they needn't keep repeating "how to…etc." They should adapt the title to their subjects. A singular subject would require the article *a* and a plural subject would not require the article or a final *s*, both in parentheses.

The language of the poem can be quite free. In fact, inspired by my students, some years after writing "A Rose Knows," I decided to write a book of poems about colors as seen in a city in which the "knows" is implied, not stated directly. Now I often read one of these poems along with "A Rose Knows," to show students another, freer version of my original idea. I've included one of these poems ("White") here in case you would like to try this approach, too. You can present both alternatives at once or in sequence, depending on the level you're teaching.

White

White spatters streets
With pigeon droppings,
Splatters the sky with stars,
Slips through your window
With thin fingers of moonlight,
Stretches out on sheets
And pillowcases
And never sleeps.

White rises from subway gratings,
From cooking pots
And ice cream cones,
From vacant lots
Where dogs dig bones,
Wherever snow drifts
And fog lifts.

White doesn't show its colors
On a crayon or a brush.
It seems to have no hue,
Not even a blush
Of pink, a touch of blue,
Or green's pale shadow.
Yet it holds a spectrum,
A hidden rainbow
That without a prism
Is lost to our sight,
Blinded by White.

But when raindrops fly
On a sunny day,
White's colors may,
As they run across the sky
Or a building full of glass,
Take your breath away.

—Orel Protopopescu

Model Poems

Ocean

The ocean knows how to swim
From one side of itself to the other.
It knows where to find the shores
It loves to meet.
It flows with the wind,
Runs with whales and fish,
Likes to ride its waves.
It waves at the sun
And teaches itself how to survive.
Surrounding islands,
It plays with dolphins,
Eating away at the shore.
The ocean loves when people come
    to play in it
And it hates when they leave
Because it feels sad and lonely.
It loves to make new friends every
    day—
People, sea creatures, seaweed, and
    ships.
It hates when people make litter
And throw it in its body.
It sleeps when people leave the
    beach,
Dreams of traveling all the way to
    Pluto,
Searching for other oceans,
And coming back to find a cleaner
    planet.

—O'Connell/De Marco classes,
Wood Park Elementary (2nd)

REVISION NOTE: I prompted some revision by asking questions. "And what else does it know?" I kept asking throughout this process. "Where does it swim?" I asked after the first line, prompting the second. "What does it play with? Eat?" I prompted, reminding the class to include various verbs written on the board. I also asked why, as in "Why does it hate when people leave?" or "Why would it want to go all the way to Pluto?" That last question led to the concluding lines.

Yellow

Yellow knows how to write.
Yellow hides among the clouds,
inside the sun, and gets mixed up when
yellow and blue make green.
Yellow wants to rest in the window,
making it warm.

—Ryan Roehrig (2nd)

Gold

Gold knows how to shine
like a diamond or a firefly.
It knows how to hide,
in the soil and in the rock.
Gold knows how to survive
the chisel and the drill,
the cold and heat.
Gold knows how to live
forever through fire or ice.
Gold can live for years and years
without going black or blue.

—Momin Malik (3rd)

The Wind Knows

The wind knows how to kiss your cheek,
blow when the sun is up,
and comfort the weeping willow.
The wind knows how to play with your hair,
dream with the stars,
and play with the sun.
It feasts on the clouds and sips sunshine.
It lets you know when it is there.
The wind really cares.

—Rachel MacGregor (4th)

T-Rex

A T-rex knows how to jump and make
rumbles in the earth
and he rides a triceratops
all day long.
A T-rex knows how to steal
the life of its prey,
how to sharpen its teeth
and to whip its tail like a rope.
A T-rex knows how to cry
and how to sing the dino rockabye.
A T-rex knows how to write
on trees with his fierce claws
and how to floss his teeth
with trees.

—David Malangone (4th)

Laziness

Laziness knows how to live.
It knows no boundaries, from TV
    to sleeping.
It knows nothing, not feelings, not
    craziness.
Laziness knows my name.

—Anonymous (7th)

Darkness

Darkness knows
        hunger.
It knows when to gorge itself
on the sweet, yellow light of day.
It knows when to nibble
at the bottom of daylight's skirt
        and then,
        when noticed,
        devour the rest.
Darkness then slowly
    slides over the land,
    its yellow stomach
glowing brightly deep within.
When darkness reigns,
a million little crumbs of silver
        light it missed
    dance and sparkle
    to remind us that
        morning
            will
        return.

—Megan Orosz (8th)

REVISION NOTE: "Darkness" emerged virtually as
written. I merely suggested the substitution of "it" for
"darkness" before "missed" and the preposition "to"
before "remind" instead of "and."

Weeping Willow

Weeping willows know how to cry.
They know how to sway back and forth
in the wind. They never look up,
they always look down.
Weeping willows always look sad,
but I do not know why. They always
seem to leave remains of their green tears
wherever they stand.

—Michelle Smith (6th)

Poetry From Paintings

For this lesson, which I've tried in grades 3–12, I use art reproductions. When using postcards, I divide my stack (purchased in museums) so that small groups of students can go through them together and each student can choose one to write about. The advantage of using postcards is that each student can study one at his or her desk. The advantage of using large posters is the pleasure of sharing different responses to the same work.

In one school the art teacher supplied us with huge reproductions of paintings. We chose three for each class and allowed students to write about any one of the three. It was fascinating to see the different poems inspired by the same pictures. The poem (page 37) on Rene Magritte's *The Return* (a painting that shows a bird whose body is a day sky flying through a night sky to its nest) came from that school.

I usually begin by showing a large reproduction from a book. One I have used often is Paul Klee's *Nocturnal Flowers*, which you can find in many books on his work or you can order a poster-sized reproduction from several online sources. I walk around the room and ask the students to tell me what they see, in one or two words. The Klee is an abstract painting with floral and fern shapes, a rocket-like red object, an upside-down daisy, and a crescent moon, in which all these shapes seem to swirl around a large black dot, slightly off center, the way objects swirl around a drain. It's a colorful painting, so as I walk around, students often say the names of the colors or shapes, "red," "blue," "flower," "moon," "fern," etc., though some give more intuitive responses like "underwater" or "confused." After everyone has had a chance to look and comment, I read this poem by one of the original members of my writing club:

Once upon a night,
An artist painted a poem.
It was blue.
Everybody admired it,
Except black.
"No black?" asked black.
"No black," said the artist.
So black stomped over
and placed itself
in the middle.
Black was so heavy,
green, yellow, pink and rocket red
plants fell in, until
the artist came
and put canvas
under the paint.

—Adrienne Lu (5th)

After reading the poem, I walk around the room with the painting again and ask, "Now do you see it another way?" I explain that the poet has remade the painting in words, made it into a struggle between colors and shapes. "I want each of you to remake a painting in words," I tell them, "so we see not only what anyone can see looking at it, its colors and shapes, but also *what only you can show us*." Those last six words are essential. Repeat them as often as necessary.

 Students' writing about paintings will not necessarily use metaphors, but will tend to if the examples you read them are rich in metaphor. Andrew Attiya's "The Dove of Day" (page 37) is a wonderful model of how to extend a metaphor, since throughout his poem Andrew describes the day as if it were a bird.

A postcard of Goya's *Giant* inspired Erica Engstrom's poem "Bewildered." The Goya shows the back view of a huge naked giant at the ocean's edge. The metaphors "toenail of moon" and "muscles like rolling hills" naturally arose from the student's perception of the sepia-toned print.

*B*ewildered

(Inspired by Goya's *Giant*)

A wondering man stares
back into space
at universes beyond where
a toenail of moon hangs
crooked by a single thread.
He perches upon his ocean domain,
thinking, muscles like rolling hills
crushing sand into thin air.
The waves can't compete
with his great body.

—Erica Engstrom (6th)

The Lips of Fire

(Inspired by Kandinsky's *Improv. No. 27: The Garden of Love*)

Kiss the plain,
scorching hot.
Please, Rainmaker,
bring rain!

The unfortunate woman
in the teepee
does not know
for she is sleeping.

Her poor dog
warning her of the fire
was struck by lightning, flood,
leaving blood.

The pet bird
the woman kept
has flown away
while she slept.

The sun is falling
in the sky,
melting, melting,
losing height.

The woman wakes up
only to find
she's the only one left
of her kind.

Disaster, destruction,
what happens after?
The repair work,
done without laughter.

—Jessica Noviello (4th)

The Dove of Day

(Inspired by Magritte's *The Return*)

Where early morning
And late night crash
The Dove of Day flies

It flies and sings
The song of the day
It sheds the feathers
Of the sun

The wings of
The Dove of Day
Flap away the night
And beat out the fire
Of the moon

When the Dove of Day
Has thrown away the night
And put dawn in its place
It returns

To its brimming nest
On the edge of night
The brink of day

—Andrew Attiya (5th)

Time Transfixed

(Inspired by Magritte's *Time Transfixed*)

Who's driving this train?
Where did it come from?
A train under the mantle,
Is this a toy or what?
How small this train,
I think it's come
From another world.
They'll teach me how
To walk on mantles.

—Takeshi Mimura (8th),
ESL student

Poetry in Motion

I got this idea from the old song that comes from an even older expression. The New York City transit system used this phrase to describe the poems that adorned the subways, which were literally in motion, day and night, though they were not necessarily poems *about* motion. The idea here is, quite simply, to take any subject at all and describe it in motion.

 Start by reading aloud this (adult) model poem.

Waterfall

Water falls
Apart in air
Hangs like hair
Light installs
Itself in strands
Of water falling
The cliff stands

—Samuel Menashe

Point out to your students the clever way Menashe breaks the title word in the first line into noun and verb, continuing the idea in the second line. Also, note the evenness of the lines with their rhyming echoes, rhythmic as water falling. The poet keeps adding more details to the picture: first the falls, then the way it hangs "like hair," then the light installing itself "in strands" which seems to refer back to the hair, but surprises us by spilling over into "Of water falling" in the next line. The solidity of the cliff behind the falls is the final detail, a seeming after-thought that literally "sets" the fluid scene.

 Share the model poems on pages 39 and 40. They have different subjects, but they have more than motion in common. These poems break down complicated motions into smaller units and they slow time. It's important to stress that poetry in motion is *slow* motion. That is, although the action described may be quick, the poet must take the time to describe it in detail, guiding the reader step-by-step. Choose the models that suit your students' ages and interests.

Explain to your students that the subject of their poem doesn't have to be a concrete object like a basketball or a leaf. They could describe the motion of a feeling passing from one person to another, as in some of the student models. It could be the changing motions of a cloud or of a face registering varied emotions.

If a student is having trouble coming up with a topic, I offer words from the word box. These are the same nouns I use for the "I Am" and Voice poems found on pages 29 and 30.

Model Poems

 ## Leaf

It rides the air,
twists
to catch a current
that soothes
its rough edges,
its spiraling
downs and ups,
shows
its flickering faces,
first, a green shining,
then a pale matte,
twirls
in doodling loops
as the sharp blade
of its tip
carves
a floating track
until Earth
lays it flat.

—Orel Protopopescu

DISCUSSION: What are the "flickering faces" of the leaf? How does Earth lay it flat?

 ## Footsteps

Footsteps turn and twist,
crunching soft sounds all around.
All shapes and sizes step
like wind blowing everywhere.
I feel happy when I hear
footsteps dance.

—Blair Silvestria (4th)

 ## Pen

A stick figure takes off a skinny hat,
makes a dive-bomb for the paper.
Lines form a word, POETRY.
It shoots back, then hovers a minute,
making an invisible trail.
It creates squiggles to shape a story
on top of the paper with a fast drying
     blue ink.
It blasts upwards, puts on its hat,
and floats back to its den
to sleep.

—Sara Morey (4th)

 ## Blast Off

It rumbles
like an earthquake,
burning energy.
Flames rise
as it begins to hover,
then redder it glows,
as if anger grows
inside its dark heart.

—Steven Biamonte (4th)

REVISION NOTE: These poems were hardly changed. A few unnecessary words were taken out of each for rhythm. Sara replaced the verb *goes* (which she used twice in her original version) with the more active verbs *shoots* and *blasts* and added the words *to shape a story* after I asked her to give a reason, silly or serious, for the squiggles.

Waves

Feeling the waves beneath me,
I glide over the bay,
A green quilt that covers me.
I hear the thump of my heart,
A rush of excitement through me.
When the waves calm down,
My heart will slow down,
Feeling them roll under me.

—Elizabeth Anger (5th)

Nightfall

The night falls
on the city,
black lacy sky,
shimmery stars,
ravishing moon.
As moon shines
on the window,
I can feel
the beam of light
on my skin.
I can see
the shapes moon makes
when clouds float by.
They remind me
of dogs, bunnies,
other furry animals,
and my mind drifts softly
as I fall asleep.

—Nicole Maningo (5th)

REVISION NOTE: Although *shimmery* is not
in the dictionary, I suggested Nicole exercise
poetic license and keep it.

The Manta Ray

The giant manta swims
gently through the sea
with huge black speckled wings.
The sun shines off its back
like a mirror on a wall.
It lifts its enormous body
out of water, flies through air,
and splashes into the sea
like a playful dolphin.
As you watch him,
you become relaxed
by his gracefulness.

—Frankie Fodera (6th)

It Can Fly

The ball cuts,
Slices,
Dances to the song of
Flight
And spins.
It rips and
Curves,
Soars like
Feathered wings.
It dances to the
Song it sings
And then it
Drops.

—Keith Manfre (8th)

Poetry, Chinese Style: Writing Shi

This lesson grew out of my work on the book *A Thousand Peaks, Poems from China*, coauthored with Siyu Liu. Our dual-language book on Chinese poetry and history features my translations (and Siyu's word-for-word transcriptions) of 35 poems in the classical *shi* style spanning two thousand years of Chinese history. *Shi* is the Chinese word for "poetry" and the form is explained in detail on the reproducible on page 42.

Make copies of page 42 for your students and discuss it before they write. I recommend that you also read aloud some of the model poems on pages 43 and 44.

Give your students at least 15 minutes in class to write a poem. Tell them you would like them to try to follow the typical *shi* structure, as much as possible:
1) image
2) change of angle on the subject
3) thoughts and/or feelings

Tell students they should feel free to use more than four lines. Explain that they can move closer to their subject, looking at one detail, for example, or move away from it, seeing it as a small part of something much larger. The change might be a change over time (seeing the subject before and after some event), a change in point of view, a change in the weather or mood, even a change of heart. At first they might describe something or someone they dislike, but then tell about something they admire about the subject.

Students might trade papers and make suggestions on one another's work before reading their poems aloud. You may notice that some of these poems rhyme and others don't. Some use the typical *shi* formula and others don't. A strict formula is not the key. More important is freshness of perception and feeling. You may wish to write along with your students, as this teacher did.

Reminder
Waves of rain break by my window
driven by fierce autumn winds.
On a St. Bart's terrace, the valley
  disappears.
How near my memories hover!

—Ann Bohlin (teacher, 8th)

Poetry, Chinese Style: Writing Shi

Shi is the Chinese word for "poetry," but it also refers to a particular style of Chinese poetry. The simplest *shi* poems have:

1 Five or seven Chinese characters per line and four or eight lines. Each character is a word. Rhyme was often used, but poems that once rhymed now may not, because of changes in the way words are pronounced over the centuries.

2 In a typical four-line *shi*, the first two lines paint a clear picture for the reader.

3 The third line gives a twist, a new point of view on the subject.

4 The last line expresses the poet's thoughts and/or feelings.

The following poem, "Willow Song" (from the book *A Thousand Peaks, Poems from China,* by Siyu Liu and Orel Protopopescu) is a translation of a seven-character-per-line *shi*. Read the poem several times. Notice the "twist" in the third line and the poet's fanciful thought in the last line.

Willow Song
From the clear green jade of one tall tree,
ten thousand green ribbons hang silkily.
No one knows who cut out the thin leaves;
perhaps the wind-scissors of February.

—He Zhizhang (659–744, Tang Dynasty)

The tree is described as if cut from jade, a precious stone that is often green. Its branches are "green ribbons" that hang down like silk. Its leaves are so thin, they seem to have been sliced by the wind. In the Chinese original, the wind is "like scissors," but here the simile is translated as a metaphor, "wind-scissors."

Study this poem; then try to write an original *shi* in English. You don't have to rhyme or count syllables, but make your English verses rhythmic. Paint a picture (with words) of anything in the universe in the first two lines (a person, a landscape, a rocket traveling through space, etc.), look at it in a new way in the third, and give your thoughts and/or feelings in the fourth line.

Model Poems

Remember that the most important factor in writing a *shi* is to offer an idea/feeling based on close observation.

Outdoor Concert

Twittering wings fly up, down,
left, right, tirelessly rearranging,
as if never satisfied with the music
they write on the telephone lines.

—Siyu Liu

Apple

Apple, high above, not knowing
the burden of its own weight, falls.
From the ground, looking up,
apple can feel the shade.

—Maureen O'Neill (8th)

Rain

I hear you walking in the day
as if dancing on a cloud.
You are a scholar of music
until you drift away.

—Lauren Wyckoff (8th)

Drum

Sticks stroke, one by one,
leaving a loud sound.
Attracted by their swing,
I dance aloud.

—Kevin Jackson (8th)

Taxi

Unmellow yellow
Garish chariot kicks its fumes.
Inside, each tick tock
Drains my wealth and health.

—Richard Barnhart (teacher, 8th)

Sunset

Blues, pinks, purples, and yellows mix
   in the sky.
Slowly, they disappear into another set
   of time.
Lonely, I am left on top of my bed,
until the evening we meet again.

—Ezgi Kirisciogli (7th)

Fall Mystery

Yellow, Red and Orange fall like rain,
Their tree homes stolen by wind.
Why must only evergreens stay awake?
A mystery of Fall, answered by Spring.

—Gemma Martinelli (6th)

Birches

Birches, bare, rustled by cool winds,
Peaceful as winter approaches.
A note cuts through, a blue jay's song,
I think, so soft, yet strong.

—Tori Sarant (6th)

My Fire Tree

The green giant stands tall and strong,
Its branches grabbing the sky.
Now it turns yellow, orange, and red,
And down the fire-leaves fly.

—Brittany Tomkin (6th)

Play

As the red curtains separate,
The tension in my heart leaps.
In the audience, I see my family
And some of my butterflies fly away.

—Olivia Fowara (6th)

REVISION NOTE: This student revised her poem in class. She graciously agreed to share her first draft of the poem, so you could see how my suggestions helped her improve it:

As the red curtains separate,
The tension in the cast's heart leaps.
In the audience, I see my family.
Hopefully, it will be a good play.

I liked the idea of the cast having a heart, but thought that having two voices in such a short poem (third person and the first person) was confusing. I suggested she rewrite the entire poem in the singular "I" voice, especially the last line, which was not as strong as the rest. "Focus on the body," I told Olivia, "the way you began. What happens to your body when you see your family?" She answered my question with the wonderful line, "And some of my butterflies fly away." A great revision, on the spot!

Thunder

You pound upon my door at night
With fists of stone, big and bright.
We see you as a frightening light
But miss you when you're out of sight.

—Jessica Wright (5th)

Rules

Rules are meant to be broken,
As a baseball shattering glass.
In my heart I know what's right,
And when to put up a fight.

—Melisa Celikoyar (4th)

Twilight

I look up in the sky,
A blur of red, yellow, and pink.
The sun and moon whisper their secrets
Before they go their separate ways.

—Katherine Koehler (4th)

Puppies

Puppies run in circles,
So fast they can't stop.
No one knows how they get that power.
Perhaps it's the love in their lives.

—Brianne Flanagan (4th)

Without

A desolate, empty place,
So alone, cold, afraid.
Are you inside or are you out?
I am trapped within; I can't stop time.

—Julian Kocheer (8th)

Found Poems: A Shi Writing Game

Writing games are a wonderful way to liberate the creativity of reluctant young poets. I was inspired to create this game by the precise structure of Chinese poems in the *shi* style.

On page 47 words from the poems in my book, *A Thousand Peaks, Poems from China*, coauthored by Siyu Liu, have been printed and their parts of speech indicated. Photocopy them, cut them out, and paste each word on an index card. Keep them in separate piles, all verbs together, all nouns, all adjectives, and all connecting words. For simplicity, conjunctions and prepositions are grouped together in that last category.

Tell students they will be creating an original poem by interpreting the meaning of words dealt at random, as if they were translating.

Shuffle and deal the cards out in a pattern of four rows with five cards across each row, in the shape of a twenty-character *shi*, making sure to use all parts of speech once in each line and nouns twice. Avoid putting two nouns side by side. Try using parallelism by having two lines follow the same pattern. Vary the pattern slightly in the last two lines. See the box below for a suggested order.

Read the found poem aloud and write it on the board. Read it aloud again, but don't interpret it. If it seems impossible to make any sense of it, you may try removing the problem words (up to one permitted in each line) and seeing if you can find another one in the stack that fits better. Each student will write an original four-line *shi* based on his interpretation of this found poem, as if translating it from Chinese.

Reassure your students that there are no "wrong" ways to interpret a found poem, since they are not translating from a true original, but they should follow the same methods as they would in making a

adjective	noun	verb	connecting word	noun
adjective	noun	verb	connecting word	noun
verb	noun	connecting word	adjective	noun
verb	noun	connecting word	adjective	noun

"true" translation. Explain that since Chinese has no pronouns or inflected verbs, indicating tense, they can choose whatever tense or voice (I, you, it, etc.) they wish. Some words could be changed into nouns or verbs, or they might want to use synonyms for others. They can add articles or connecting words as they need them and change the order of the lines.

Share these words and "translations" based on them with your students.

close	peak	chase	out
rooster	late	river	scatter
into	horse	stir	head
where	fragrant	cloud	splatter
butterfly	underneath	kind	rain

> We've peaked. No longer close.
> I've chased you out, Mr. Rooster.
> Out into the late night where the river
>   stirs
> and scatters like running horses.
> Underneath a fragrant cloud,
> a kind rain splatters my butterfly head.
>
> —Jacqueline Raven

> The closer I came to the peak,
> the farther the rooster chased me out
> into the late river
> where I scattered the horses
> and my head stirred fragrance into the
>   clouds.
> The splatters of butterflies
> fell up from underneath
> in a new kind of rain.
>
> —Megan Hubel (8th)

> Close the peak and chase out the
>   rooster.
> The horse scatters into the late river.
> Stir where the head cloud is fragrant.
> Splatter butterflies underneath the
>   kind rain.
>
> —Emily Krollage (5th)

Make copies of page 48 (which explains how to do this mock "translation") for your students. Let them warm up by writing their own "translation" of this found poem. Reading aloud or sharing copies of the poems on this page would also be helpful.

You may find your students enjoy the game so much they will ask to play it again and again. Ask volunteers to read their poems aloud and enjoy the many ways of "translating" a found poem.

NOUNS

head	leaf	rain	cloud	moon
fly	shadow	mountain	tower	sun
lake	pearl	horse	wind	sky
earth	boat	rooster	storm	feather

ADJECTIVES

fragrant	silver	cold	golden	lush
late	freezing	sunny	dying	careless
close	ancient	blue	wild	clear
foreign	green	red	kind	lonely

VERBS

wither	bloom	jump	chase	enter
guide	pass	splatter	float	pretend
fly	drink	stir	sing	carry
gallop	know	scatter	find	move

CONNECTING WORDS

into	who	among	below	then
out	and	by	for	still
underneath	away	down	but	at
where	when	on	toward	as

Name _____ Date _____

Making Pretend "Translations"

"Found" poetry is poetry that is discovered by accident (for example, by selecting or highlighting words from a newspaper or advertisement) or created by random events. In this game, you will pretend to "translate" a found poem. Your teacher or group leader will shuffle and deal words in a pattern that resembles a four-line *shi* poem that has five characters in each line. Read the words and then interpret them by writing your own "translation" in four to eight lines. Feel free to add articles or other connecting words as you need them and even to change the order of the words. Below are some sample translations to give you an idea of the range of interpretations possible with the same set of words.

green	snow	find	away	leaf
ancient	time	guide	and	shadow
sing	egret	when	silver	boat
float	oriole	among	foreign	pearl

Here are several "translations" that resulted:

Snow is green where it finds wandering leaves,
guided by ancient time and its shadows.
Egrets sing when, like silver boats,
orioles float among foreign pearls.

—Orel Protopopescu

I scrape away the snow to find a green leaf,
a guide and shadow of ancient times
when we floated in our silver boats,
foreign pearls among the egrets,
singing our oriole song.

—Jacqueline Raven

In the green snow find the runaway leaf.
Let ancient times guide you into the shadows.
Sing of the egret when in your silver boat.
Float like an oriole among foreign pearls.

—Claire Nicolas White

Riddle Poems

These poems can be written in first or third person. In first person, they can sound very much like voice poems. The idea is to define something without naming it, giving enough sensory details that readers can guess what the poem is about. If they can't, then the poem may need further work. The idea isn't to mystify, but to make the ordinary seem extra-ordinary by evoking it in poetic language.

May Swenson's poem, "Living Tenderly," describes a turtle, or perhaps a tortoise, in a series of metaphors. It can be found in Swenson's book of riddle poems, *The Complete Poems To Solve*. The poem is one that all students in grades 4–8 have no trouble solving. To begin this lesson, read it aloud.

Living Tenderly

My body a rounded stone
with a pattern of smooth seams.
My head a short snake,
retractive, projective.
My legs come out of their sleeves
or shrink within,
and so does my chin.
My eyelids are quick clamps.

My back is my roof.
I am always at home.
I travel where my house walks.
It is a smooth stone.
It floats within the lake,
or rests in the dust.
My flesh lives tenderly
inside its bone.

—May Swenson

Another poem you may want to share with your students is Emily Dickinson's "A narrow fellow in the grass," number XXICV in her *Poems, Second Series*. In this poem a snake is described, but never named.

I often start with a group poem to warm everyone up. Before choosing a topic for your class to write about, read this poem aloud and let your students guess the title:

Raindrops

The clouds are our home.
We leave when we're cold,
Falling like light snow,
Bungee jumping from the sky,
Feeling wind against our faces,
Hitting the ground one by one.
The sun drags us up,
Floating gracefully,
Back to our home,
Safe, cozy, and warm,
Tucked into our fluffy white beds,
Dreaming of cool winter winds.

—Mrs. Carley's Class (4th)

The following poem was clearly influenced by the group poem, which was written by this student's class. In fact, her first draft began with the same first line, "The clouds are our home," which I suggested Katherine rewrite. She decided to use the cloud imagery later, when she described lightning as "candles flickering on the clouds."

Angels

The sky is our home.
The raindrops are our tears.
The lightning, our candles
flickering on the clouds.
The thunder, the gate
of heaven opening and closing.
The sun holds our smiles.
The stars are our eyes
looking down at you,
waiting and wishing
for you to come join us!

—Katherine Koehler (4th)

 In her first draft, Katherine had described the thunder as the sound of angels bowling. I suggested she come up with something more original, which she did by replacing bowling with the glorious sound/image of "the gate of heaven..." Even students this young can recognize cliché as something they've heard before when you point it out. I was astonished by the wonderful revision Katherine did so quickly.

 I left the titles out of some of the model poems on pages 51 and 52 so your class could enjoy guessing. ("Open me up..." a book; "The gentle breeze..." a willow; "I see the world" glasses; "A mind without..." nothing; "It is the monster..." fear) Discuss the metaphors and similes used in each poem to describe its subject. To help students having trouble choosing a topic for a riddle poem, you can use the words for "Voice" and "I Am" poems. You may need to have them write the topic somewhere on the paper, in order for you to help them revise. Sometimes their poems don't contain enough clues. Encourage them to add more sensory details if you can't figure out the topic. It usually doesn't enhance the poem to end with a question such as, "Can you guess what I am?" After they've completed a draft, suggest they give the poem an intriguing title that doesn't give away its subject. Students love reading these poems aloud and letting classmates guess.

Model Poems

Open me up and I'll bring you
to a whole new world.
I'll take you on an adventure
without ever leaving your home.
In me, you'll find the present,
past, or future.
I can make you smile,
laugh, frown, or cry.
Sometimes, I am very old,
passed down from generation
to generation.
I am like a song
with no sound.
I hold thoughts,
stories, and poems.
When you close me,
I bring you back
to your own world.

—Hayley Bogue (4th)

At the Pond

A swollen lily pad
Grew eyes, a tongue, then
Left a hole in the air
Where a fly had been.

—Orel Protopopescu

Fast Trip

Do you want to travel very far
yet never leave your home?
Look through me. I'll take you out
past whirling stars that tell
their stories made of light.
Peer into my glass eye
and feel yourself shrink.

—Orel Protopopescu

The gentle breeze blows
As if tempting me.
The fierce winds push,
But apologize later,
By giving me fresh rain.
My fingertips touch the ground.
My slender body holds me up.
My friends in the sky
Always keep me breathing and alive.

—Annie Verdino (5th)

Who Am I?

My habitat is in the water,
my skin a winter's snow.
To you my innards beat
like the wings of a unicorn.
Little space I take up.
inside my tank, I sleep.
And the croaking sound I make
is a trademark all my own.

—Diana Ventigmiglia (8th)

Feeling in the Wind

The king of beauty,
rider of the wind,
can you hear the stomping of his feet
and see his coiled horn?
Can you glimpse his white hair,
feel peace in the air?
But when you look again,
there's nothing there.

—Megan Mackenzie (6th)

I see the world
Through the eyes of others
Because they can't see
As well as me.
My life is hard,
But I don't mind,
Because I am blind
Without people.

—Brian Jones (7th)

It is the monster in my closet,
the shadow on my wall.

It appears in my unconscious mind
as I toss and turn at night.

It can be my friend,
warning me,
preparing me for danger,
or it can be my foe,
tormenting me with things
that aren't there.

It is the crying child,
lost inside my soul.

—Melanie Honercamp (8th)

A mind without thoughts
A pen without ink
An untraveled road
A chain without links

A universe undiscovered
A vacated room
Words without meaning
An ungiven doom

This Earth without life
A toothless comb
The Sun without rays
The rest of this poem…

—Susan Redman (8th)

Recipe Poems

This poetry lesson asks students to write a recipe, using the language of cookbooks, for something you could never use a recipe to make. I have seen variations of this idea in several sources, but not elaborated with the specific details I suggest here. It generally works best if the topic chosen is abstract, not concrete: a recipe for love, for peace, for friendship.

✺ Explain to students that they will be writing a recipe poem. Read one or two of the sample poems on pages 54 and 55 to them. I've selected several from grades 4–8 to inspire your students.

✺ Provide students with a copy of the reproducible on page 57. Also provide them with the list of possible topics found on page 58. You may want to duplicate and cut up the words to use in the word box (see page 20).

TEACHER TIP

Students, of course, should not be forced to use any words they pick, but some find it oddly freeing to have the choice made for them. It takes away the stress of having to decide. The approach may seem formulaic, but the fill-in form is just a way to brainstorm for ideas. Students then select those they like best and develop them. The work this technique yields is surprisingly rich, often humorous.

✺ Supplement the topics I've listed by asking your class for other possibilities, such as a recipe for curing shyness or any of the world's ills, for getting what you want, for flying without wings.

✺ Recently I attended a conference with writers from *Sun Magazine* where I met the poet Sparrow. At an evening reading, the following poem was rewarded with convulsive laughter. Sparrow agreed to let me share his recipe for "memory milk" with students and teachers. I was not sure fourth graders would get it, but those I read it to laughed as heartily as the adults:

Memory Milk

Place 3 raisins, a square of chocolate and 2 Cheerios in a cup of milk. After 5 minutes, strain the milk and drink it.

Note: The milk contains the "memory" of the raisins, chocolate and Cheerios.

—Sparrow

The humor comes from thwarted expectation. One expects that "memory milk" is a drink to improve memory.

Model Poems

Recipe for a New Star

Take some sight and touch.
Put them in a bowl.
Mix until lightly blue,
until a lump of sadness comes through.
Drop in friendship and some hope.
Cook at 40,000 degrees
until it forms a star shape,
moving slowly.
You can tell it's done
when it's sparkling wildly.
Let it stand and cool
until jade green comes in.
Sprinkle on a glitter of happiness.
Bring it up into the sky.

—Mariana DeMarco (4th)

A Recipe for Friendship

Take two lonely people
and add a cup of jealousy,
one cup of forgiveness
and two cups of fun.
Mix until a thick bond of trust appears,
then add three-quarters of a cup of
    sugar.
Test friendship with hate and disbelief.
Add sleepovers, pool parties, and
    laughs.
Let stand till unbreakable friendship
    appears.
(Try to test bond.)
It tastes of success, hope, and joy.
(This recipe works almost always.)

—Patricia Varady (5th)

Recipe for a Little Brother

Take a person who talks like a parrot
and repeats everything you say.
Add shoes that he ties himself.
Mix a checkers board and checkers
with people in a family.
Warm with hugs until
a golden brown heart appears.
Let it cool until you're ready for playing.
Add a little bit of learning.
Taste a bit of friendship.

—Lisette Alexander (5th)

A Recipe for Tears

Take your fears, a cup of pain,
and a lost loved one.
Put them together in your soul
and mix them with each other
until your eyes start to water.
Then you'll see eye drops,
water from your eyes.
Cook them all, with large degrees of love,
until you know you're crying.
You can almost tell when they're done
when you feel them slipping and sliding.
Add a lot of love, cut it up
into thin slices of water.
Doesn't it taste like tears
running down your face?

—Nicholas Esposito (5th)

Recipe for a Beautiful Mom

Take half a cup of lip gloss,
one teaspoon of blush,
a drop of mascara,
a cup of natural beauty,
and a half cup of eye shadow.
First, mix the lip gloss, natural beauty,
and mascara for one minute,
then pour all ingredients
into a large bowl.
Mix with a golden diamond wire whisk
until smooth and creamy.
Let it stand.
You will know when it's done
because it will start to form a mom.
When it is fully done,
you will have a beautiful mom
standing next to you.
Serves only one child.

—Nicole Joines (5th)

Recipe for Invisibility

Take three cups of air,
two cups of hot water,
and one suit.
Put the suit in hot water,
then add the two cups of air.
Mix with a big spoon
until it disappears.
Place on a hanger to dry,
then put it on
and you will disappear.

—Kenneth Pikoulas (5th)

The Creation of an Angel

Begin with an eternity of peace,
A ray of sunshine, and two moonbeams.
Pour into an ocean of love and hope,
Then stir with a crescent moon until
She sparkles like the stars.
Now sprinkle with the softness
Of a baby's skin.
You must leave her on the windowsill
For five heartbeats so she can feel
The love and warmth of the world.
Serve on a platter of white clouds
With a side of feathered wings.

—Marisa (6th)

Recipe for a Great Grandmother

Take 2 cups of kindness,
A teaspoon of sharing,
Another of caring.
Mix it all in a blender,
Then put it in a bowl.
Next add 5 cups of love,
A cup of old age,
And pour in some wisdom.
Throw in a full-sized heart.
Don't forget a half-cup of wrinkles!
Stir until it turns white
Like the color of her hair.
Pour it into a woman-shaped pan
And cook in an oven at 500 degrees.
After an hour you'll hear chuckles.
Let it cool until you see
An aged woman
With cookies and milk
Just for you!

—Sarah Conde (6th)

Recipe for a Dream

Take two cups of cloud,
one billion stars,
one cup of moon,
three cups of sky,
and shake them up
until they fly high.
Pour in a rainbow
with a bit of heaven,
cook it in your mind
at just the right degrees,
until you fall asleep.
You'll know it's done
when you see the perfect dream.
Let it stand to cool
until you wake up.
Sprinkle on some fairy dust,
serve with a smile.
The taste? A happy child.

—Krisanne Ocedek (6th)

How to Make Revenge

First you take two heads
full of tension and anger.
Mix the two together
To make a black substance
with a foul smell.
Mix in a good idea
and a world full of violence.
Plan far ahead before serving.
No cooking is required,
since revenge is a dish best served cold.
Revenge should be sweet for the giver
And bitter for the receiver.

—Chris Vallone (7th)

A Recipe for Failure

Begin with just enough force to wreck a life,
a pound of danger,
blend with too much confidence
and a lifetime worth of rage.
Let sit for twenty minutes or until dark.
Pour on excuses to top it off.
Let sit, do not heat
or you will lose the bitter taste of defeat.

—Kevin Ulrich (7th)

A Recipe for Divorce

Start off with one whole husband
and one whole wife.
Add sixteen cups of hate
followed by one separation.
Throw in a court and a judge
followed by two lawyers.
Let it bake in a courtroom for a week,
then cool with the tears of children.

—Pat McCaffrey (8th)

A Recipe for Love

You need
two cups of passion
half a cup of caring
and a tablespoon of friendship.
First, mix the passion and friendship
with a blending spoon very well
until they're stuck together like a kiss.
When you feel the friendship and passion
have caressed, add the half cup of caring
and mix it all together until
it is like one big hug
and you have made
a pound of love.

—Danielle Jacoberger (8th)

Name _____ Date _____

Recipe Poems

Use this form to brainstorm ideas. Then choose the best ones for your poem. You do not have to include every step in the final poem and may add others not on this list. Some recipes may not call for heat, for example. Use what works best for you.

Take _____(ingredients)

_____

Put _____ (ingredients you need to combine)

In _____(receptacle)

Mix (or blend, stir, chop, etc.) with (utensil or machine)_____

_____

Until _____

_____ (how you can tell it's ready)

Pour (or throw, drop, etc.) _____

_____

Cook (bake, broil, fry, etc.,) in a _____

At _____ (temperature) Until _____

_____

You can tell it's done when _____

_____

Let stand (cool, etc.) until _____

Add (sprinkle on, etc.) _____

Cut (slice, chop, etc.) and serve (with, to, etc.) _____

Taste _____ (result?)

loyalty	art	hope	purity	mistakes
abundance	theater	divorce	amnesia	illness
joy	good	marriage	heroism	destruction
family	music	magic	bliss	dreams
confusion	revenge	rage	pollution	fear
love	growth	smile	corruption	madness
hate	memory	ruin	winter	jealousy
genius	evil	friendship	spring	vacation
faith	truth	heaven	fall	sanity
sorrow	energy	party	summer	noise
happiness	bedlam	tears	talent	silence
maturity	war	death	decay	greatness
beauty	success	gratitude	unrest	femininity
stardom	peace	eternity	protest	sweetness
laziness	taste	winning	justice	nerve
poverty	overwork	losing	mercy	betrayal
dance	wealth	cool	sleep	boredom
poetry	failure	mothering	health	masculinity

Revising Poetry

I've included revision notes for some of the model poems in the book. Often students' poems required only minor cuts, not worth noting. In this section I've included drafts of several poems based on my lessons, along with my revision suggestions. You may want to make overhead transparencies of some of the drafts and final poems so you can discuss the process of revision with students as a class. On page 64 is a list of revision guidelines for you to share with your students.

"What You Mean to Me" by Ali San Roman

Ali San Roman wrote this poem in response to one of my metaphor lessons.

I loved the first draft, but suggested Ali consider substituting other fruits/ vegetables for "avocado" and "pineapple." A heart can be squashed and a tongue can be tart, like a lemon, but I had trouble picturing an avocado ear or pineapple lips. I suggested she try other body parts, such as "soul" or "cheeks" or "hands," etc. She answered me by mail sending four versions of her poem, but based her final selection on this reasoning, as she wrote me: "I took your advice and decided to use another body part, instead of ear. I put in hand, and a cactus can hurt a hand, just like when you break up with somebody, they hurt your heart (hence you're the squash of my heart). I decided to keep in you're the pineapple to my lips because if you think about it, pineapples are prickly, and if you bit into a pineapple without peeling it, your lips would hurt an awful lot. I'm not sure if the line 'You're the love of my life' should be a statement or a question…"

She tried "You're the love of my life?/ Then why are you the onion to my eyes?" We agreed this didn't work, since the last question was not appreciably different from the previous statements. Here is her final draft.

First Draft

You're the avocado of my ear.
You're the squash of my heart.
You're the lemon of my tongue.
You're the pineapple of my lips.
You're the love of my life.
Then why are you the onion to my eyes?

Final Draft

You're the cactus to my hand.
You're the squash of my heart.
You're the lemon to my tongue.
You're the pineapple to my lips.
You're the onion to my eyes.
Then why are you the love of my life?

"waiting" by Amanda Burris

I asked Amanda for permission to publish her poem in a book for teachers and she graciously allowed me to use her rough draft, too. As I explained to her, I wanted to include even her misspellings, not to make her look bad, but to demonstrate that spelling well and writing beautiful poetry have nothing to do with each other. Amanda's poem is full of deeply felt, original, and surprising lines. Many of them were written in response to questions I asked as she wrote. I'm offering her rough draft here to show you how I work with a student to choose the best lines for a finished poem and to expand on them.

In this draft, I put the parts I suggested Amanda cut in italics. Why did I feel she should cut those lines? They seemed to me not as original as the rest, more like the platitudes you find in greeting cards. Once Amanda added all those vivid details, describing the narrator's friend, who needed these generalities that could apply to any friend? Her particular friend, as described in her own words, is so much more lively and appealing.

First Draft

every summer you come and say Hay
you make me happy
although your not here, I heir your voice
saying my name (* I suggested adding description here, "I see...")
I write your name on my hand waiting
every summer to come and cuttle I
can not come down to visit my scegwal
is to hettic but there always
time for you

> *you an your sister are the best*
> *better then the rest you were blessed*
> *with a good friend let this friend ship*
> *never end*
>
> *what I say every day*
> *when I wont see you again*
> *one love*

*additions: (This is what she wrote after I asked for more description)

and I close my eyes and see your brown
eyes and between the top of the nose bone and the right side of
the eye there is ....(alternate: and when I close my eyes I see your bright brown eyes and
between the top and corner of the right side of thy eye there is) a beauty mark his
light completion of
your skin
your taller then me wider then me
our love is beger anof to see

—Amanda Burris (6th)

Here is Amanda's final draft. I was impressed by the vivid details she had added.

Final Draft

waiting
every summer you come and say Hey!
you make me happy—
although you're not here, I hear your voice
saying my name
and when I close my eyes I see
the light complexion of your skin
your bright brown eyes
and between the top of the nose bone
and the right side of your left eye
there is a beauty mark—
you're taller than me, wider than me
and our love is big enough to see—
I write your name on my hand, waiting
every summer for you
to come and cuddle—
I cannot come down to visit
my schedule is too hectic
but there is always
time for you…

"Nearing You" by Katie Chun

"Nearing You" was written in a Poetry in Motion lesson. Katie Chun made several cuts in her first draft. The poem describes a swirl of turbulent emotions within the narrator that changes when a loved person draws closer. Compare the final version of the poem to her first draft below. Words eventually cut are in italics.

First Draft

Heart skips a beat
A tremble in my mind.
It almost feels like falling.
But I can't see anything around me
Or feel a past emotion.
Memories swirl *through*
My mind.
It's almost like running
Away from my heart.
But everything catches up
And suffocates me *so*.
Then it all stops.
And the pain is *all* gone.
You stand there with
Warmth
And an outstretched hand...
(Rest as in final version.)

Final Draft

A tremble in my mind
feels like falling.
Memories swirl,
like running away
from my heart.
But everything catches up
and suffocates me.
Then it all stops.
The pain is gone.
You stand there
with an outstretched hand.
My hand dances to yours
and a smile that was hidden
is found.

"Ribbon" by Elizabeth McCarthy

I've included two drafts and the final version of the next poem which was written for my Poetry in Motion lesson.

First Draft

It starts flat
with no destination
The first lift
of the two ends
A tight knot
Then the beauty
The loops perfectly
wound and even
Finally, it's an image

Second Draft

It starts flat
with no destination
the first lift of the sides
the tumbling waves entwining one another
the pull that makes it all disappear
into a knot.
Sadness, because
the sea cannot last forever
Feeling the silk rubbing gently against
   your
fingers.
You slowly create two perfect hills which
as you cross the two and pull again
drain the remorse from you as you
discover the image of a bow.

Third Draft

It starts flat,
with no destination—
Then the first lift of the sides,
the tumbling waves entwining one another
and the pull that makes it all disappear
into a knot.
Softness on softness, as your
fingers glide on the ribbon sadly,
because the silken sea cannot last forever.
You slowly create two perfect hills,
cross the two and pull again,
draining your remorse
for crushing a soft body
as you discover the image
of a bow.

Ask students what they think has been gained with each revision. What (if anything) was lost? The word "remorse" is a strong choice. Ask them if it works for them and to explain why or why not. Is this poem just about making a bow or could it be a metaphor for something else?

"Recipe for a Dream" by Krisanne Ocedek

The final draft of this poem appears on page 56. Her first draft is below. I had suggested that Krisanne Ocedek cut the references to "heaven" and "rainbows" in the first part because she repeated them in the second part where I thought they were more effective. I thought she should take out the part about putting the stars, moons, and clouds in the sky because how could one pour them then or shake them until they fly? I felt that the first part of the poem was undercutting the second in the first draft.

Also, some grammatical irregularities were fixed. For example, "cups of clouds" doesn't sound right, because ingredients are generally listed in the singular. I also addressed the problem of voice, the use of "a child" and "you" intermittently. Krisanne decided to use "you" throughout, except at the end. To say "the taste is a happy child," might sound too literal.

First Draft

Take two cups of clouds, one
billion stars, one cup of moons,
three cups of sky, four cups of heaven
and five cups of rainbows,
put the stars, moons and clouds
in the sky, shake them up until
they fly high. Pour in a rainbow, with a little bit of heaven,
cook it in a child's mind just
at the right degrees, until
you fall fast asleep. You'll
know when it's done when
you see the perfect dream. Let
it stand to cool until you wake
up, sprinkle a little fairy-dust
on, serve with a smile,
the taste is a happy child.

One could argue that in smoothing out inconsistencies, one loses the child's voice, a danger I do recognize. But I've found that children's voices are not lost to revision. If that were the case, all the poems in this book would sound like mine. I only wish I could write as well as many of my students! My own poems have inspired far better ones. That may embarrass the poet in me, but it delights the teacher.

However, if you prefer that your students edit their work without input from you, I suggest you have them read their first drafts aloud to the class. Very often a student will hear an unnecessary repetition that they didn't catch when reading silently. Ask your students to delete words they don't need words that don't allow the poem to breathe.

How to Rewrite Your Poems

1. Read your poem aloud, listening to the rhythm of your words. Take out extra words you don't need.

2. Break lines where it sounds right to you, or looks right, or emphasizes what you want to say. Each line does not have to be a clear grammatical unit, but make sure you know why you're breaking your lines the way you do.

3. Check punctuation and capitalization. Do with or without either, but don't change the way you use them halfway through your poem unless you have a good reason.

4. Does your poem flow from line to line or do you want a choppy effect? If not, see if you can find new ways to make the poem flow by changing or adding words.

5. If you use rhyme, don't let it use you. Rhyme shouldn't force you to say things you don't mean, but help you to say what you didn't know you meant. Try to use surprising, unexpected rhymes.

6. Be specific, not general. Give clear pictures of what you mean. A rose is specific. A flower is general.

7. Are all your lines in the right places? Try moving ideas around.

8. Do your words make clear pictures for the reader? Instead of telling us something is good or nice or pretty, show us what makes it like that. Let us see the picture in your mind when you use those words. Then you may not need them. Circle all the adverbs and adjectives. Do you need them? If you couldn't use these words, what other words would you use instead? Try circling all the verbs, too, especially *is* and *was*, to see if you can think of stronger ones.

9. The best ideas come from the work. You don't have to know what you want to say before you write or rewrite. Discover this as you work. As the writer E. M. Forster said, "How do I know what I think until I see what I say?"

10. As the writer Grace Paley said, "Write what you don't know about what you know." How? By imagining it in another way. For instance, you know what a baseball is, but what does it feel like to be a major league player? To be the last person on Earth who remembers the game? To be the baseball, flying through the air? Surprise yourself and you will surprise your readers too.